Snap

Dion N. Farquhar

Snap

Poems ©2017 by Dion N. Farquhar
all rights reserved by the author

Cover photo taken by the author
at the San Francisco Museum of Modern Art

Crisis Chronicles #93
ISBN: 978-1-940996-44-8
1st edition, 1st printing, 100 copies

Published 31 August 2017 by
Crisis Chronicles Press
3431 George Avenue
Parma, Ohio 44134 USA

crisischronicles.com
ccpress.blogspot.com
facebook.com/crisischroniclespress

For Alex, Matt, and Marsh

Table of Contents

Chronic Edge. 1

Humanities 2.0. 3

Break. 4

Difference Within 6

Path. 7

Contingency 8

Branded. 9

Lost 11

Unsustainable 12

Loopy. 14

Zuccotti Park. 15

New Year. 16

Climate Change. 18

Acknowledgments 20

Chronic Edge

They tell you it's painless. You might see a bright light.

No worries. It's all good. But …

    banks begging for bailouts
    multiracial rednecks in suits
    companion robots
    running the country
    no alternative
    that's the *neo*

here comes the *liberal*

    fuck the same sex, even marry,
        now medical insurance
       for six percent of the sixty
   smoke yourself silly
   post, share, forward, and cite all night long
   make all the music you want
   digital recording equipment now affordable

individual   *objectivity*   *contract*
   the new *a priori*
stealth, cunning, and self-congratulation
exile irrelevant
the red manicure against the yellow chipped chalk
acts of god up my alley like an *Oklahoma!* tornado

    Jud alone in the smokehouse
        it was the reach that axed him

new friend for a month, then silence
being dropped hurts but no one to cry to
if you're not on Facebook blogging every second
the default loneliness
what did I do wrong

→

       mangy dog   grotesque
       at the heart of desire

choice
between checking out
with PayPal or Visa

Humanities 2.0

Are there still things
outside commodities
ecosystems outside markets
      body exceeding bed
      streets the house
      spaces the store
      stars the city
          sorcery the straight
work devouring
foregrounding backdrop
      thinking
still
      neck and neck
      with feeling
      knowledge
not Googling (like AI)
10 K answers in point 3 seconds
surface/depth one big algorithm
logos pathos ethos
      dead to branding
      investment without return
consideration
      unknown except as a legal term

Break

> What is the end of study,
> let me know
> —*Love's Labour's Lost*

life measured in time off
the global model
work as punishment   forced
to till the ground from whence he was taken

pumpkins, witches, turkeys, and trees
        a world crawling with tropes
hard on the heels
of the two-month respite, summer

disguised as someone else
I drive one son to music camp
past the brown valley of the San Joaquin
oboe and countertenor
Erfreute Zeit im neuen Bund
centuries before German
was the language of the camps

I have read too much   never enough

so speeded up now: modular high-rise education
interchangeable zeros and ones
even the *New York Times* notices
the incompatibility
of universities and advanced capitalism
        library hours slashed   layoff mayhem
        the seminar extinct
        the non-instrumental bumped to the basement
all this for rocketing fees, crowded classes

fundamentalisms burgeon
like the Saudis   coexisting with high-tech
we sign our licenses   pony up our organs
when we die in a head-on

the right to study
to not be immediately useful
an anachronistic frivolity
      loafers losers leeches
luxury communism
the very idea
dare not speak its name

there's a bee on the tree
outside my study window

      a city   friends

traded for

      good weather   space

a round trip ticket to New York
something worth going down for

Difference Within

only the tips of pines, tops of eucalyptus trees
the rest obscured by structures
    the greater the dependency the greater the power
        agoraphobe-claustrophobe couple
    what is love anyway
    a fantasy chase   dictated by a daimon
    obsessive circulation   disavowal
raised in exile   no kingdom to reclaim
    closest kin our cruelest foe
    they lose, you lose
    they win, you lose
the sister is not a mister
prescient odd essentialist
    not that apple, not that door
    women dying to know
piledriver pounds a beam into the ground
emitting a small cloud of smoke with every clang
spits two quick clouds: on one side, a small one
        a larger on the other
    indoor plumbing inevitably accompanied
        by a world of useless shit

illuminate your page, not your partner
with a bright, cool halogen recessed light

Path

The more's a knowledge double-edged
compounding dilemma with scarce time
tracking depths, interiors scanned,
worshipping at the altars of actuaries
    Buddhas of the boundless
    moments precious
    nothing taken-for-granted
    the small powers
—to pee, swallow, listen to music

Lives racked up like most
choice shrunk to a hope or dream
    staying home
    going out
better to die trying:
struggle the heart,
there is here
later becoming now,
anxious genuflectors
to Sloan-Kettering
nomograms

Contingency

Was it a movie about keeping the bête noir at bay or a TV series about another fuck-up single dad who means well and makes good or was it the real life memorial service for the high school junior stabbed to death downtown at 10 on a Friday night or could it have been the president's decree to commence offshore drilling or was it seeing Lady Gaga playing piano on your iPhone that established how out of it one can be in myriad niches though certain local knowledge is unshaken like it was exactly a year after the Black Belt test and three years after you set out to be a psychoanalyst, commuting monthly to LA and it was the long slow privatization of the schools, endless pizza fundraisers to keep the music program going or maybe it was when the lazy Sunday afternoon went into overdrive when the dog running full tilt after a ball caught his dew claw on a tuft of grass and came limping, wimpering back, foot cascading blood, emergency surgery, anesthesia, bandages for his poor paw, and for a week the photo of us from ten years ago with the boys reaching up to your waist sat on the desk in the guestroom along with the rock from the shore and it was the Monday after the Sunday water aerobics class when you walked through the door at the airport pulling your carry-on behind you at the renovated robot airport and now you're at your summer cottage on Lake Michigan and by Tuesday the house felt empty despite a partner and two kids who are mostly on their computers playing shooter games and even the cappuccino machine felt lonely about a country split down the middle and me, still a committed tea drinker minority, on the left seam of it, another contingent faculty not rehired, not even counting as a layoff ...

Branded

epistemic promiscuity
doesn't get you very far
    better than default defeatism
      to be or not to be merchandise
        not always on top
        not always hard

switch it up   or back
      the anchor   the potter's wheel
      calculate eclipses
      chart the solstice

always a fundamental ambivalence
about labor

    I dream a lie   but why

      Kyle sends me an email promotion
        about a free movie
          in St. Louis
  I texted the woman it was targeted to
      whom I didn't know
     she told me she couldn't go
    because she was going
to a wedding and Friday was the rehearsal dinner
    I went home and emailed K
       subject line:
      I'm depressed

family like empire
complicating migrancy
broken   before its break-up

in your face this life death
M's prostate cancer downgraded to a Gleason 6
milestone: a cup of caffeinated tea

→

fifty thousand Londoners in the streets
       and Rome   Bologna

for the right to study   to know our world

    everywhere but here

bled to death with cuts
    every day
    a cross-country ten-mile hike   uphill

a new condition
    enters the lexicon

        multiple role disorder
        robots preach
        work-life balance:
            internal and external conflicts
            resulting from maintaining
            a highly effective state in all self-assigned roles

        white women
        yesterday's eunuchs
        bridging the gap
        between despots and slaves

fantasy structures method   *Good Tidings to Zion*

pub as in public   or published
exoskeletal detritus
data mining   nuclear donors

      I am AFK
      long enough to fold the laundry

        blueberry picking at Earl's
        seven miles south on Blue Star
        Sandy in Chicago for Gertrude's 95th
        leaving us at the Cottage
        mosquitos big as alligators
        hours of sunsets on the beach

Lost

for Mike and Veronica

Raising her glass
one friend toasts:
   To the Revolution
another, Russianologist:
   As Soviet dissidents used to say:
      To Lost Causes

while wavering about
cause
you think
lost
says it all

besides
we're all
lost causes in a way
but carry on

by the election
we're islands of incredulity
theocracy advancing
with googling prescience

critics marginalized
cutbacks the new norm

instead of burning down the big house
servants on smart phones

Unsustainable

> O brave new world,
> that has such people in 't!
> —*The Tempest*

before I knew *bubkis*
lip-syncing to the whine
    faux choice, lost possibility
    the door that led to the wall
from Aeschylean angst to no exit
picking up the bone to bash
Strauss' *Zarathustra* booming in surround sound
    oh, to be a bee
    or an apple gene
    a church mouse even
    or a giant tortoise
    candle on one's back
    lumbering through the sultan's
    ornamental gardens
even Disney admits
the lushness of a bug's life
comes to no good end
    Who knows where the time goes?
no good beginnings either
    narcissistic mothers
    alcoholic fathers
animals and robots lack
    lament, childhood,
    poor things
catch-up another
Horatio Alger carrot
for better and for worse
    hip replacements, prosthetics
    the Internet, tulips
lucky dogs learning parlor tricks
for responsible owners
    cleared equals empty (as in decks)
        days free to sit in libraries
            when they were open
            when there were books

        remembering reading
        when there was time
salvation dies hard
the dialectic double-edged
not betting on 10,000
years of co-evolution
to get us anywhere

Loopy

Passengers awoke one morning
to find that the airport
had inexplicably
turned into a corporation,
years of construction unveiled
by sweeping spaces
the exterior 400 meters
of giant undulation
benign bird but robotic to the core
all beckoning in
pointillistic shades of grey

dimly lit Greeting Area
"Arrivals" board small
barely legible
a matrix of sub-electrodes
but on the walls
three-deep, banks of four across
plasma-leeching flat screens
their liquid crystal brilliant
blues fill an entire room:
> *Easy Migration*
> *Control Your Data*

male voice a serious saccharin
> *baseball bats, golf clubs, and torch lights*

balancing business critical
> *exception for breast milk*

a deliberate spoken muzak
> *cell phones, money clips, large metal buckles*

robotic reassurance
> *straight razors, and sharp, pointy scissors*

affectless cadence
> *knives, cutting tools like box cutters*

children are not required to present identification

Have an enjoyable and a safe trip.

Zuccotti Park

always already
on the side of the damned
while ruing the need for sides
    one and one do not equal three
even when golden multipliers say so
    enacting law as nature
        while bleeding both

the commons   along with free time
now Lilliputian islands
        yet still
        savoring   simmering
    the delicious now: glow of an onion and tomato tart
        the way it is
in between   epiphany and ash

there's no one in the cockpit
    so commandeer the galley
    cookies for the main cabin

we had too much going on
to live there, camp out
    a pinched nerve, learning to play the oboe
    doing our PT exercises and oh yes,
    indenture to the fucking jobs
    we're so grateful to have

students   loafers   crazies

made the time, slow-cooked a wondrous spectacle
hope bursting through their blogs:
unstable zones unfolding *en plein air*
    food   shelter   medical   security
    a functioning library
    open til midnight

frighteningly free
like the fire
in the nostrils of the bull downtown

New Year

> *Ev'ry valley shall be exalted.*
> —Handel, *Messiah*

1. *Arise*

champagne, glitter, confetti
    the stupid hats
inexorable yuletide countdown
thrumming pull-back
the mounting commercial convulsion
surf sucking every shell and pebble out
    a happy cover story
    frozen
    to the calendar
        a babe's born in a manger
            resistance is futile
        yet the ground of being
            of even having a soul
            not fully adjusted to capital
            accountants and juntas
    is negation

2. *Behold*

New Year's Eve
soulless though "live"
the ball dropping
broadcast annually
to a globe wracked
by disappointment

3. *Rejoice*

    Times Square millions
    waving homemade signs
    Occupy! We are the 99
    we are fruitful and we morph
        Newark, the Columbia quad, a Baltimore mall
        Chicago's Board of Ed, Oakland's Port
        Boston Occupy its own radio station

stacks of speakers
democracy a living thing
General Assemblies
in the freezing cold

General Assemblies
in the freezing cold
public spaces and parks
again accessible

4. *The dead shall be raised*

Carving life, *being*,
from something already lost
but valiant, necessary
imagining the not-yet

just-in-time socialism
an end to surplus suffering
valuing process over product
the most vulnerable protected

only then

and we shall be changed

Climate Change

Hard to feel
        no divination

hard to know
        double-edged   bloodless coup

touch
        mostly memory

slow violence
this anthropocene:

        injury invisible
        fragile biosystems
        austerity   deregulation   mega-mergers

untallied
disposable
impossible to source

        locavore wannabee

        sitting
              thanks to ibuprofen

crying at my electronic screen

Acknowledgments

Climate Change – *Local Nomad* (Summer 2015)
Contingency – *Ping Pong* (Spring 2011)
Difference Within – *Local Nomad* (Summer 2015)
Path – *Wonderful Terrible* (Main Street Rag Publishing, 2013)
Unsustainable – *Local Nomad* (Summer 2015)

www.ingramcontent.com/pod-product-compliance
Lightning Source LLC
Chambersburg PA
CBHW071805040426
42446CB00012B/2715